An APOLOGY from TRUMP'S AMERICA

Inspired by Plato's Apology

An **APOLOGY** from **TRUMP'S AMERICA**

Inspired by Plato's Apology

Tony D. Senatore

Foreword to
An Apology from Trump's America

by Walter E. Block

English departments at major universities no longer require familiarity with the works of Shakespeare on the part of their students. Why not? Did they suddenly discover that this author was a plagiarist? Not a bit of it. He is a dead white male. Speaking of plagiarism, both Martin Luther King and Claudine Gay were indeed found guilty of this most serious violation of intellectual precepts. The former is still widely venerated, while the latter, the former President of Harvard, is still on the faculty of Harvard for shame. Our great orchestras no longer play the music of Bach, Mozart, Handel, Haydn, Vivaldi, Beethoven, and hundreds of other magnificent composers. Have they suddenly changed aesthetic sensibilities after many years of featuring such musicians? Not at all. These creators of the most vital and inspiring music the world has ever seen suffer from the malady of dead white male-ism, to coin a phrase. Orchestras will continue to play the symphonies of Joseph Bologne, Chevalier de Saint-Georges, known as the "Black Mozart." His music, too, cannot be denied; it is excellent, but that is not why his offerings are still found on the stages of our prestigious concert halls. It is due to the color of his skin.

In some circles, acting in a color-blind manner is deemed unacceptable. It is almost a curse word. Why? It obviates affirmative action and DEI, and if we embrace a race-blind society, we will not have representation in industries, professions, and schools that "look like America." For some mysterious reason, the National Basketball Association (NBA) or the National Football League (NFL) has never pushed DEI and affirmative action. Do we want to cure cancer, heart disease, diabetes, or not? Do we want to set up shop on the moon or Mars? Do we want to reduce fatalities from volcanoes, storms, floods, traffic accidents, and airplanes falling out of the sky? Given that we do, we need the most talented people working on these challenges, and if they have skin colored blue with green polka dots, it should not matter.

How did we come to this sad state of affairs? Marxism, cultural and otherwise, has taken over all too many of our most important institutions. What to do about this? Fight back. One of the best ways is Tony Senatore's *An Apology from Trump's America*. He approaches the challenge from a unique perspective, not economics, philosophy, culture, history, or any of the usual perspectives. It is, instead, a unique one. The closest I can come to describing it is as poetry. It is a very powerful attempt to put things right in this regard. Read this and be inspired not to make America great again; we were never very good at that sort of thing. Instead, to put our country for once on a proper path in this regard.

Introduction

In 1962, Orson Welles brought to the screen The Trial, a film he believed to be the best he had ever made. While the film was clearly an adaptation of Franz Kafka's famous novel from 1925, Welles angered critics by downplaying the similarities. Welles argued that when an artist had something unique to say, the source material, while important, was merely a conduit that allowed the creative person to create an entirely new work of art that stands alone from the original. The key to his logic was that the artist adapting the source material needed something different and unique to say. Similarly, I have written a modern-day remake of Plato's Apology called An Apology from Trump's America. While I have primarily adhered to the original, I have deviated significantly. In my treatment, I have an older, Black American conservative (Adamantios) in the role of Socrates and a young, blue-haired feminist (Professor Fiocco Di Neve) in the Meletus role. Via a Socratic dialogue, what begins as a cross-examination designed to convict Adamantios for allegedly corrupting the youth of Columbia University with his "older ways of thinking" and preference for equality over equity and capitalism over socialism ends in a mistrial, and a dialogue in which the conservative and the feminist have a newfound respect for each other. Di Neve has the last word in a final monologue that delivers a scathing indictment on the current state of democracy in the United States and the idea that we all, like Socrates, must make it our mission to replace ignorance with knowledge

I started writing An Apology from Trump's America in 2016, and it was completed in 2020. The pandemic and the changes it brought caused me to radically revise my work. I wrote my final draft in April 2025, an eight-year journey to write nineteen pages. The most significant change was removing myself from the Socrates role and inserting the Black American conservative, who immediately becomes the enemy of the campus progressives when he disagrees with them, revealing that progressives often care more about the ideology they profess than the people they claim to want to help. I urge readers not to be overly concerned with details, as my story straddles the line between realism and surrealism. *An Apology from Trump's America* is inspired by, not based on, *Plato's Apology*, and my collaborator is Plato; there are numerous ways my words could be interpreted. I prefer that my readers come up with their own interpretations.

O, citizens of Trump's America, my detractors have done an excellent job despising me and my works and my opinions. They have deftly portrayed me as an aberrant, worthy of scorn and ridicule, in words so persuasive my mother would not know who they were speaking about. Of all the indictments made against me here tonight, the one that I find most troubling is the idea that I plan to deceive you with words steeped in skillful rhetoric and eloquence. I have not prepared my words tonight, preferring to convey my thoughts in a manner befitting a musician and Black American whose life story is a firm testament to living his faith; my worldview is a mix of capitalism, Catholicism, and the gospel according to John Coltrane. I consider myself a modern-day version of Howard Roark, but I use music rather than architecture to express myself.

Consequently, objectivism and many of Ayn Rand's ideas resonate with me. This has often caused me great hardships, as well as my pro-life stance on the abortion debate, which I will address later. Although it may be true that this is the first time I have defended myself in a court of law, I am confident that the justice of my cause will belie the deficiency of my words. Professor Fiocco Di Neve is responsible for the charges I defend myself against this evening. She represents only the most recent in a long lineage of accusers who are not present, thus depriving me of the opportunity to make my defense. In many ways, I regard the older false accusations of being an apologist for former President Donald Trump and the wisest man in America as more of a problem for me than the newer ones, as I fear they will bias the judges. For this reason, I would like to explain the older charges before I proceed to the more contemporary charge of corrupting the youth of Columbia University and that I am an enemy of democracy.

Shortly after the Presidential Election in 2016, I was introduced to Professor Cronkletus, a semi-retired college professor from New Jersey who taught philosophy and religion at a community college. While I was never his student, he had an excellent reputation as a man with great wisdom. I was honored to make his acquaintance in my final year at Columbia University. I looked forward to speaking my mind without being prejudged because I adhered to conservative and libertarian ideas, and I knew Cronkletus was at one time a conservative. Initially, I wanted to discuss my growing disillusionment with religion, specifically the sex abuse crisis in the Catholic Church. I also confessed the difficulty that I have in reconciling my self-professed Judeo-Christian values with my disdain for the caravan of immigrants who are coming into the country illegally from Central America. Inevitably, the conversation shifted to politics and whether one man, Donald J. Trump, is solely responsible for the social disintegration in today's world.

While Professor Cronkletus neither voted for President Trump nor supported him, he was upset that some of his progressive friends had called upon him to sever ties with those who voted for and supported President Trump. In our discussion, we both noted that in Trump's America, the media portrays individuals who support former President Trump as racist, sexist, homophobic, xenophobic, unintelligent, or any combination thereof; the name Donald Trump is practically an eponym for corruption. He named all his friends and associates who voted for President Trump. These included a research chemist, an insurance corporation executive, two nurses, a hairdresser, a substantial number of college professors in various fields at various institutions, two university librarians, a college administrator, a widely read novelist, a prominent biblical scholar, a Protestant minister, a psychologist, a physician, two lawyers, a CPA, a businessman, an IT engineer, and several musicians. Correspondingly, I noted that I also had a similarly diverse group of friends at Columbia who supported President Trump, which differed from the media portrayal of the archetypal Trump supporter. Still, they were all unwilling to publicize it, fearing retaliatory attacks. Cronkletus and I agreed that we would not categorize any of the Trump supporters in our circles as racist, sexist, homophobic, or xenophobic; in fact, we were not sure if we would categorize ourselves as Trump supporters.

Nevertheless, I used these conversations with Professor Cronkletus as the foundation for my ideas about President Trump, which I made public in various discussion groups connected with my sociological studies at Columbia. Unfortunately, my professors could have better received my ideas and said my views expressed what they believed to be an older way of thinking. This resulted in the first of the older charges against me. They called me a Trump apologist and thought that saying anything positive about President Trump in any capacity was tantamount to supporting him. At the same time, many of my younger classmates would approach me after class, after some of my classroom battles with my professors, to learn more about my life and my ideas. I was equally as interested and excited in learning about theirs. Notably, they were typically from a wealthier class than I and infinitely better educated. All I had to offer them was my public school education and a lifetime of experience that laid bare the fact that the theories professed in academic circles often fall apart when encountering the complex world we live in. Because of these after-class dialogues, some students rethought their intransigent stances regarding who was misleading the youth, whose influence should be ended, and who the dangerous ones in society are.

And now, O men of Trump's America, I would like to address and dispel the second of the older charges against me: the idea that I have developed a reputation for great wisdom. Many of you are familiar with my friend Dulcemadera, a rabble-rouser who fought the good fight for conservative principles while a student at Columbia University. As you might remember, he was brought up on charges of gender misconduct for calling himself handsome in his Chinese language class in 2014. Dulcemadera was somewhat impulsive in his actions, and one day, this led him to visit the oracle in the ivory tower at Columbia University and ask whether I was the wisest man in Trump's America. The oracle responded that there was no man wiser than I. As I argued earlier, I have never made any claims to knowledge, preferring instead to display the ignorance of my interlocutors. Thus, I found myself in a quandary: the oracle could not lie, yet I was convinced I had no wisdom or specialized knowledge. Henceforth, I set out to refute the assertions of the oracle in the ivory tower by engaging with those in Trump's America who I believed possessed greater wisdom than me.

I sought out the activists, who were held in the highest esteem by most of the professors and academics I had encountered at Columbia. One of these activists, in particular, had a reputation for possessing great wisdom and, like me, was a person of color. He also attended Columbia University, a prestigious Ivy League university, and was the first person in his family to attend college. Even though he was granted a full scholarship, he frequently posted on his University's Facebook page that he hated America, a nation he asserted was built on genocide and white supremacy. However, most of all, he hated the University he attended and criticized it publicly and privately. When I told some classmates about my disdain for this particular activist's message, I was mocked and criticized by most students and administration members who agreed with him. I met with this activist whom the students and administration regarded as the spokesperson of all Black activists. I informed him that he neither spoke for me nor the legions of Black Americans who have been able to fulfill Columbia's Core Curriculum requirements without claiming that reading the words of white European male authors is tantamount to perpetuating racism and sexism.

Regarding achieving full equality for Black Americans, I told him that if blacks want to walk with dignity and be truly equal, we must realize that white people cannot give us equality. It is not something that can be handed over to us. Although the activist I engaged with owed everything to the good nature, generosity, good wishes, and decency in the American people's spirit, his decision to criticize America rather than praise it proved to be a better strategy. He ultimately received a scholarship to pursue graduate studies at Cambridge. His essay about how America failed to acknowledge its systemic racism and white supremacy cinched his acceptance. I decided that my quest to move towards a world where no person's worth is based on race or gender, while stressing the universality of our humanity, was a better plan for me. The type of activism that my Columbia classmate prefers and is so prevalent today has had a corrosive effect on America and calls into question the outstanding achievements of Black Americans who want to and can compete on equal footing with anyone and do not wish to have a university's standards lowered for them or to disparage their country.

My encounter with him made me realize that when considering who speaks for Black America, his message of victimhood and hopelessness has become the predominant voice in America's institutions, thus squelching any possible alternatives. Many of my peers believe this particular activist is a race huckster and has crafted his stance for personal gain and profit. Others looked upon his worldview as limited and ignorant and thought he would benefit from hearing different perspectives from Black and white Americans alike. After my conversation with the activist, I realized that this man seemed wise to many human beings and, most of all, to himself, but he was not. As I left, I reasoned about myself: I am wiser than this human being. Probably, neither of us knows anything noble or good, but he supposes he knows something when he does not.

Next, I went to the progressive politicians, who were

revered in Trump's America, especially among young and impressionable college students, but also a significant part of the baby boomer population. I met with the most popular progressive politician, a female known as OCD. I told her I considered her well-intentioned plans more harmful than beneficial. True racial equality seeks to de-emphasize immutable characteristics, such as skin color. Relying on white Americans to administer equality isn't a satisfactory option. As James Baldwin asserted in Nobody Knows My Name, it is demoralizing when the lives of Black Americans are "dominated by the power of white people in the name of paternalism," and that even with the most humane and charitable actions of "superiors," such an arrangement denies the "subordinate class" of an "essential element of human dignity." Sadly, modern-day politicians advocate affirmative action, reparations, diversity, equity, and inclusion policies. I asserted to her that these policies foster a victim mindset while simultaneously inflaming racial division and that it was possible that racial turmoil in the United States across the United States would result from these social engineering experiments.

Before long, it was apparent that these politicians preaching this nonsense were some of the highest-paid individuals in the United States, and as Milton Friedman asserted, "preaching equality and promoting or administering the resulting legislation had proved an effective means of achieving such high incomes." Thus, I concluded that the oracle was correct. I might be the wisest man in Trump's America, not because I am more knowledgeable than others, but because I am unsure. Others are less wise than I am because they claim to know things they do not know.

Finally, I went to the journalists, hoping to refute the oracle's statement that I was the wisest person in Trump's America. I recall the turbulent times of the Vietnam and Watergate eras and how responsible journalism, steeped in courage and delivered with minimum partisanship, made journalism one of the bedrock institutions of American society. At the behest of my most learned friends, I listened to the pundits they deemed most wise; you may know them from the cable news networks. I initially believed that they were more pretentious than they were wise and seemed to employ many tools of dissimulation. This was designed to keep the American people from better understanding the issues that affected them the most. Even so, I continued to listen, hoping for a conscientious and impartial examination of the facts, but one was not forthcoming. The unwillingness of activists, politicians, and journalists to put their hatred aside for Donald Trump, a democratically elected President, has resulted in a defect and derangement in them that overshadowed their wisdom, a syndrome with no historical precedent. This defect made me realize

I possessed neither their knowledge nor ignorance. Thus, I realized that some men and women who held high esteem were the most foolish, and some considered deplorable, were often wiser and more venerable than those revered in society. Moreover, it was evident that the oracle was correct and that I was the wisest man in Trump's America because I do not think I know what I do not know.

Confident that I have defended myself against the charges bestowed upon me by my more ancient accusers, I will now address the more contemporary charges against me by Professor Fiocco Di Neve, the Dean of Columbia University and a practicing attorney. What are the charges? Something along the lines of that is that I, Adamantios, am a corrupter of the youth of Columbia University and hostile towards democracy. Professor Fiocco Di Neve says that I am the corrupter of the youth, but I say, O men of Trump's America, that she is unwittingly doing the corrupting, and I shall endeavor to prove it. Before doing so, I would like to speak on behalf of the late Dean Peter Awn because, in many ways, he is responsible for the positive aspects of what is happening here today. For those unaware, Mr. Awn was the champion of non-traditional students like me who had whole lives and careers before setting foot on a college campus. When I felt unworthy of being a Columbia student and told him I was blessed to have been accepted to such a prestigious university, he turned it around. He told me that Columbia University was blessed to have me as a student. Awn believed students like me would add a necessary counterweight to the left-leaning agenda at the University.

Moreover, he thought students from my generation would benefit from hearing excellent solutions to our time's great moral and ethical dilemmas from the younger students that we never would have considered. He warned me that not every faculty and student body member would be as welcoming as he was but to persevere through any adversity. If not for his belief in me, I would never have made it to graduation.

Having sufficiently defended myself against the first group of my accusers, I want to focus on the second group led by Professor Fiocco Di Neve since she has made it her mission to accuse me of corrupting the youth of Columbia University and portray me as an enemy of democracy. Come forth, Professor, and let me ask you a question. Do you think much about improving the student body of Columbia University and the youth of America in general?

[**Professor**] Yes, I do.

In that case, please tell the judges presiding over my trial who improves them. Since you have decided to ridicule and destroy me publicly, you must have ideas about who improves them.

[**Professor**] Our laws improve them.

That is not what I am asking. I want to know precisely the individuals you speak of.

[**Professor**] The judges, Adamantios, who are present in this courtroom.

All of them, or only a few and not the others?

[**Professor**] Only the judges with progressive inclinations

And the senators?

[**Professor**] Once again, only the progressives.

Please elaborate on your criteria for deciding who improves and elevates the youth in what you refer to as Trump's America and who corrupts them.

[**Professor**] The corrupters of Trump's America are the conservatives, the political party that continues to deny that America was built on white supremacy and systemic racism. They hold antiquated views, which I find reprehensible, hence the "older ways of thinking" quote.

Can you be more specific?

[**Professor**] You mentioned many of them in your opening. Let's start with your pro-life stance. You have the audacity to believe that you and other men have the right to tell women what to do with their bodies, like your desire to overturn Roe vs Wade.

Let me be very clear about something. First, the idea that the abortion debate is centered around the concept of men telling women what to do with their bodies is absurd and inaccurate when thirty-three percent of American women oppose abortion. Second, when I say that I am pro-life, that is precisely what I mean. When possible we must strive to choose life whenever possible. Despite your desire to make generalizations about people who don't share your worldview, I was not happy when the Supreme Court turned abortion over to the states. There is a rumor that you said non-traditional students like me at Columbia gained acceptance through the back door. As a Black- American, I take offense to the analogy. You do not know a lot about me that you should. Did you know I was in an interracial marriage and held the Columbia University banner and that I marched down Fifth Avenue alongside the Dean of the School of General Studies, representing Columbia University at the Pride Parade? Are you aware that I had my 90-year-old mother move in with me so that I could take care of her?

[**Professor**] Yes, I heard all of those things. Still, that does not inoculate you from the charges that you might be a racist, hostile to the LGBT community, and an evil person making a concerted effort to cultivate a favorable public persona. As you stated in your opening, you made a living as a musician. It follows that someone like you, who speaks of capitalism with reverence and derives inspiration from someone like Ayn Rand and Howard Roark, would represent all that I despise, but go on. Why did you wait so long to pursue your college degree?

My sister had a long history of mental illness, drug addiction, and alcoholism. When she unexpectedly got pregnant in 1993, she knew she would be unable to raise her child properly. She discussed possible alternatives with my family, and ultimately, my sister decided to have the child with the knowledge that my mother, father, and I would raise her. From 1993 to her high school graduation in 2011, I was a mother and a father to my niece. When I felt I could ease up on my parental responsibilities, I enrolled in college in 2008 and graduated in 2017. So, it is evident that there is a lot of nuance to the idea that I am pro-life. Perhaps saying that I was pro-choice would reflect my views more accurately and quell some of the hostility directed towards me, but I prefer to refer to myself as pro-life. I understand that in certain circumstances like rape and incest, abortion is sometimes permissible, and we can both agree on this point.

On the other hand, can you understand that some believe that abortion is never morally permissible under any circumstances? Moreover, millions of women are pro-life, which makes it clear that it is not only men who oppose abortion. As a result of Roe v. Wade, abortion was once legal in all fifty states. Pro-lifers, many of them women, were not happy about it, but they abided by it, and that is one thing. Asking these same individuals to support abortion and institutions like Planned Parenthood, which go against their religious beliefs with their tax dollars, is entirely another. I can say with absolute authority that raising my niece as my biological child to help nurture her and witness all the beautiful things she has done in her personal and professional life has been rewarding and the reason I was put on this earth. I strive for a world with fewer, rather than more, abortions.

[**Professor**] I heard a rumor that in your first year at a different college in 2008, you debated a young female student regarding whether abortion should be legal. Naturally, you chose the pro-life side of the debate. While I don't know the particulars of the discussion, I know that you reduced the girl to tears as she bravely defended her pro-choice stance. I know that she ran from the classroom, and you ran out after her, and the class was dismissed, and the matter was never brought up again. I have always thought that you were particularly monstrous for your actions that day, and I am glad to get the chance to expose you for what you are to the faculty and student body at Columbia. I resent men who think they have the right to interfere with a woman's health decisions, and I believe I speak for all women.

I am delighted you dredged up this story from my past, relying on secondhand sources and hearsay. Thank you for giving me the chance to set the record straight. When my classmate ran from the room, I ran out the door after her. I asked her if I had said anything to traumatize her, and if so, I wanted to apologize. It was at that moment she confided in me that as she stood before the class to debate me, she was two months pregnant, and the father of her child had abandoned her. I told her my story of my family and raising my niece and my mom, who worked until she was eighty, to help me support her. Neither my sister, family, nor I believed in abortion. That notwithstanding, despite an old professor calling me a moral relativist, we felt every woman had the right to choose, especially in a world where conservative politicians implore women to carry their pregnancies to full term regardless of whether they are raped or the men who are responsible for making them pregnant abandon them, then deny them resources when they try to raise the children alone. I hoped the story of what my family and I did for my niece would inspire her and give her direction. I embraced her, wished her well, and never heard from her again.

One day in 2013, I received a call from a number I did not recognize, but the name was familiar. As it turns out, it was the girl I debated in 2008. She wanted to tell me that my story dramatically altered the course of her life. She took a few years off from college but was now a year away from her nursing degree. She said that although the man responsible for making her pregnant abandoned her, she decided to explore motherhood. With help from her mother, father, extended family, and friends, she was a mother to a five-year-old son who was the center of her universe.

[**Professor**] I am glad being a mother worked out for your former classmate, but motherhood is not for everyone. It is not for me. Moreover, if I ever had a change of heart, adoption is a viable option.

How old are you, Professor Di Neve?

[**Professor**] I will be thirty-three years old this coming December. Why do you ask? Are you going to lecture me about how entitled, coddled, and spoiled people from my generation are? If you are, please spare me. It is reassuring to know that you and everyone who thinks like you will soon be dead. I know that sounds harsh, but I feel that way, as do many from my generation. I have no maternal instinct, nor do I want to bring a child into a world that is getting worse every day. I am sorry that some might disapprove. I am proud to be a childless cat lady. You should know that although I have blue hair, tattoos, and a nose ring, I'm not a moron who needs everything mansplained by you.

I neither planned on lecturing you nor criticizing your appearance, and it saddens me that you long for my death, but I am offering some advice you might find helpful. When

I was twenty, I thought I had the answer to everything. At every ten-year juncture, my worldview changed dramatically. I am finally starting to understand how the world works at age seventy, but I have a long way to go. Every time I was at a fork in the road and a decision had to be made, I used to think I made the wrong decision every time, with few exceptions. In retrospect, what seemed bad at the time was right for my family and me thirty years later. Raising my niece as my biological child was the most significant decision I ever made. Studying at Columbia University was the other. Here in these hallowed halls, I learned how to think for myself by respectfully countering the arguments of my professors with well-sourced arguments. I graduated from Columbia magna cum laude as a conservative black man with zero bars or standards lowered for me. I earned an accomplishment that nobody can take away from me or minimize.

Before you rule out motherhood, you should consider my idea that the experience of living your life might change your views. You might think differently ten years from now. To your point about rejoicing in my death and the end of older ways of thinking, I want to assure you that I am not going anywhere soon. I want you to know I will fight you with my words and actions. It is clear to the judge and the jury that I am interested in dialogue and learning from you and anyone in a position to teach me something, and you are only interested in destroying me. Now that I have clarified my position on abortion, I wanted to explore the Roark/Rand/capitalism connection. What is your problem with capitalism?

[**Professor**] I don't know where to begin with so many shortcomings in a capitalist system. Capitalism is a system that perpetuates inequality. In a capitalist economy, what I find most repulsive is that everything has a price. Selling your wage labor as a means of sustenance makes individuals hate what they once loved. I have a photographer friend with a portfolio of the most incredible pictures I have ever seen. She took these pictures alone, with no motivation other than creating art. Unfortunately, she can't survive by only being concerned about being creative. As a result, she is a wedding photographer and has to spend twelve-hour days with people she detests and work environments that crush her creative spirit. Finally, the division of labor necessary in a capitalist economy produces alienated workers who toil away at simplistic tasks far removed from the final product.

I see you are well-versed in Piketty's Capital, which, like the Marx/Engels Reader, is issued to incoming Columbia University students like a canteen, and combat boots are issued to privates in the United States Army. Your argument was more convincing when Marx and Engels asserted it in 1848. Let me start by saying that although you disapprove of capitalism, and I speak of it with great reverence, my ideas are much more complicated than the narrow reductionist view you wish to attribute to me. I will start by saying that although I prefer capitalism as an economic system, I do not necessarily think it is superior to a planned or socialist economy or even an anarcho-capitalist society, especially the current state of crony capitalism in the United States, which is based on soft corruption and graft.

[**Professor**] I am glad you brought that up. In addition to corrupting the youth of Columbia University with your idea that democracy has not lived up to expectations, you have been quoted as saying that using democratic mechanisms to organize society via a representative government might be unwise. You even asserted that the ideas in Plato's Republic might be better than what our Founding Fathers conceived over two hundred years ago. I hope you understand how radical this statement appears. It is the reason you stand before this court today. Additionally, you asserted to young and impressionable Columbia University students that the democracy we have in the United States is a perverted and heretical version of the ideas put forth by Plato in The Republic.

I will address my penchant for frequently promoting the ancient Greeks' wisdom. Before doing so, I would like to explain my preference for capitalism over other economic systems. Socialism, or, taken to its fullest extent, communism, is an economic system imposed from the top down rather than growing from the bottom up, as in capitalism, and usually via the barrel of a gun. Socialism is a theoretical construct so complex that the individuals who were being exploited were unaware of it and had to be reminded of it via propaganda and constant agitation. Contrary to the Marxian notion that selling wage labor as a commodity is exploitative, that is precisely what Americans love to do. I have made a living playing the saxophone for over fifty years. Whether for producers on Broadway, major record-ing studios, or touring artists, I am making a living in a manner that best suits my needs. Throughout my career, I have contemplated producing my own Broadway show and released my solo recording. Some individuals are more risk-averse and prefer to let others take the risk and, ultimately, the reward.

Your anti-capitalist stance is merely the continu-ation of a long tradition of so-called intellectuals whose knee-jerk hatred for capitalism has caused you to ignore that socialism and communism have destroyed not only economic wealth but also the mental and political freedom on which a free society is built.

[**Professor**] Capitalism is not on trial here. For the record, just because I want corporations to pay more taxes and want Medicare for all, that doesn't make me a card-carry-ing, Marx-worshipping member of the communist party. Let's focus on the matter at hand. You said to some of your Columbia classmates, many of whom are here in this courtroom, and I quote, "It is not the economic system that is the question, but man's imperfect human nature that renders all possible ways to organize society, whether we speak of democracy, communism or anarcho-capitalism, flawed." Can you explain what you mean by that and how the ideas Plato expressed in The Republic are preferable to those of Western democracies? Can you also explain your view that democracy in America is nothing more than a sinister and perverted version of Plato's Republic?

To be clear, I never said that Plato's ideas on democracy were preferable to what the United States has in place today. I merely stated that they might work if humans were less susceptible to corruption when placed in positions of power. Critics have argued that Plato's Republic is a blueprint for a totalitarian government, and there are many commonalities, such as the subordination of the individual to the supremacy of the state and the rejection of democracy. Still, Plato justified his elite rule on an absolutistic state founded on true knowledge and the eternally true essence of justice. Moreover, one set of standards could be used to evaluate all nations and cultures regarding moral forms, such as justice and courage. They were absolute, universal, and knowable with certainty, like the forms of the circle and triangle used in arithmetic, astronomy, and geometry. Plato would undoubtedly condemn as illegitimate governments that glorified a specific leader, as in fascism, or that pitted social classes against one another, as in communism.

Plato believed a city was a man "writ large against the sky." In the Republic, there was not one morality for individuals and another for the state. Cities and their governments were as natural as human beings, and the elements a city is built on correspond to the elements constituting the individual human soul. The morality or justice of the city is no different than it is for the individual.

Plato's tripartite theory of the soul asserted that the essence of man was comprised of three elements: rational, spirited, and appetitive. A human can use his mind for logical thinking, deductive logic, displaying bravery or cowardice in a given situation, or giving in to or succumbing to desires. Humans struggle to keep these three elements in check, and to Plato, nothing is more important than reason. Thus, the state and those who administered it did so based on the three aspects of the human soul. The state was a natural outgrowth of the individual and contained three different classes: guardians, military, and producers. Their temperament and roles were vastly different, but they worked together holistically. This starkly contrasted with Marx's idea that the state was a dictatorship of the ruling class and existed to exploit the proletariat and the Christian notion that the state was neither natural nor good but existed as a restraint against unrestrained human passions.

[**Professor**] I disagree that a universal form of justice and morality is knowable with absolute certainty, as are rectangle, square, or triangle forms. One culture is not better than another; it is merely different. Every society, from primitive to advanced, is unique, and no outside, universal standard can be used to evaluate them. Cultures evolved in their own ways and their own regions and periods. Moreover, concepts of morality and justice vary, depending on the culture and the individual, and the idea of absolute ethics is impossible.

I find it surprising that someone who refers to herself as a feminist and a supporter of the LGBT community and BLM could make such a claim and support countries and regimes that go against all you hold sacred while disparaging a nation and a system that best reflects the type of world you aspire towards. Tolerance and fence-sitting are in vogue today and might benefit your career at Columbia, but I think you're doing a disservice to your education by holding such views. The apparent drawback to your moral and ethical relativism is exposed "writ large," as Plato would say, with the rise of Nazi Germany and the work and extermination camps in which millions of Jews were tortured and murdered. Are you suggesting that Nazi Germany could not be judged because it was unique and evolved in its own way with its standards and values? The record of history is crystal clear that humanity cried out in the judgment of the Nazis. Of course, moral and ethical relativists get around my point by minimizing the Holocaust, or worse, asserting that it ever happened. Nevertheless, when it comes to justice and human rights, human beings share universal human standards, and individuals have a moral responsibility to judge and speak out when these rights are violated or denied.

[**Professor**] Given the controversy regarding the war between Israel and Hamas on the Columbia University campus, I would rather not discuss this publicly, as my job might be at stake. Still, your point is a good one, and I would respond by asking you why you publicly support the deportation of migrants in record numbers and the tearing apart of migrant families currently happening because of President Trump's policies and ICE. Clearly, human rights are being violated, but by taking this on, we are deviating from the reason we are here today. If Plato did not believe in democracy, and individuals had no choice as to who ruled over them, who would be the elite group that wanted to preside over what he called a "good society?"

Regarding your first point about human rights, I think you are making a false analogy by comparing the genocide of the Jewish people to the rights of migrants in the United States who entered the country illegally and were empowered by duplicitous politicians. As a prelude to answering your question about the elites Plato wanted to preside over society, I have a question for you. If you were severely ill, what course of action would you take?

[**Professor**] I would make an appointment with the most competent medical professional I could find, a specialist in their field.

You wouldn't interact with as many people as possible, whether they had medical expertise or not, and ask them what their diagnosis was and take a vote as to what you should do.

[**Professor**] That is preposterous. Who would do something like that?

Your belief that democracy is something sacred conflicts with what you just said you would do if you were ill. Why is it that when it comes to the health of the state and society, we try to solve its problems by soliciting the advice of the ignorant many rather than the wise specialist?

[**Professor**] You are talking about direct democracy. I am not talking about that. The democracy I believe in is exactly what you said. We elected worldly and wise politicians who have our best interests at heart to govern us. They are well-versed in geopolitics and economics. They are indeed specialists; elites, for lack of a better word, and are well-trained to make decisions the average individual cannot make.

Can you offer a succinct definition of democracy and why it is so precious?

[**Professor**] I assert that the pluralist conception of democracy is a steadfast adherence to the idea of a common good

26

in mind, achieved by citizens electing individuals who carry out their will. It is precious because if we are displeased with the people we elect, they can be voted out of office.

I don't agree with your definition, and neither would Hans -Hermann Hoppe or Joseph Schumpeter. Are you familiar with Schumpeter or Hoppe?

[**Professor**] No. I am not. I gravitate towards the ideas of Ibram X. Kendi and Robert Reich, but please, by all means, enlighten me.

Schumpeter was an Austrian economist who asserted that there is no common good on which everyone can agree, and even if there were one, there would not be a consensus on how to achieve it.

[**Professor**] So, there is no upward flow of opinion from the people to the government. The reverse is true. Competing elites from various political parties offer themselves and their ideas to the public just as entrepreneurs offer their goods to consumers. There is no common good. Individuals are only concerned with their narrow interests, and political elites are elected to bring them to fruition. While appealing to them for votes, these elites shape the political opinions of the electors.

That is what Schumpeter believed, but let's answer your question about elites ruling over society. Whether we speak of the United States of the past, currently, or Plato's

Republic, the elites who set economic and foreign policy believed that political action and democracy are not the business of ordinary people. As Thomas Jefferson asserted in his 1813 letter to John Adams, there is a natural aristocracy. Some individuals wield more authority and respect in society due to their superior intellect, bravery, or any combination thereof. Of course, in Plato's Republic, the idea that individuals lacked the intelligence, knowledge, and temperament needed for governing made the masses unfit to govern, yet democracy gave them the right to govern, which was unacceptable to Plato. The politicians in Washington, DC, feel the same way.

[**Professor**] What was Plato's plan to remedy this situation? He believed that democracy must be rejected, and his central idea was that until philosophers became kings or kings became philosophers, a society based on justice would not be possible. In Plato's Republic, society was ruled by an elite group of the most rational. Virtue, or proper conduct in life, flows from the knowledge of what constitutes the tripartite human soul and the ability to use all three parts in their proper harmony or order. Only those with extraordinary powers of reason have the right to exert control over the other members of society. Although he has expanded upon it, the most crucial feature of Plato's ethics is based on Socrates' statement that virtue is knowledge. The guardians possessed it and, therefore, set the rules.

[**Professor**] Please tell me more about the guardian class. Your knowledge of philosophy makes me wish I had studied more Greek philosophy as an undergraduate.

For one thing, Book V of the Republic has been noted for its defense of the equality of the sexes. Thus, women could be part of the ruler, military, and producer classes. Plato believed that governing a society required extensive training, and the rigor aspiring philosopher kings had to endure in pursuing truth and knowledge, a fifty-year process, has no modern-day equivalent. By the age of thirty, those who sought membership in the guardian class received extensive training in hopes of understanding the visible world and the intelligible world, which held the eternal truths. After a series of competitive examinations, the worthiest candidates spent five years studying dialectics, which is the highest level of knowledge. After a fifteen-year probationary period in which candidates learn the idiosyncrasies of everyday politics, they will become philosopher kings.

[**Professor**] I imagine they were paid very well for their dedication to the pursuit of truth and service to the state.

On the contrary, members of the guardian and military classes were forbidden to possess money or private property. To avoid conflict between family loyalties and their loyalty to the state, both classes lived like soldiers in barracks, with the producer class providing anything needed for sustenance.

[**Professor**] I imagine the great Greek dramatists, poets, musicians, and painters were influential in the Republic. I find more truth in the music of Bob Dylan and Pete Seeger and the comedy of Stephen Colbert and George Carlin regarding an accurate reflection of society and those that govern us.

You would be mistaken. Plato's Republic was centered on government agencies based on propaganda and censorship. The immorality portrayed by the dramatists and Homer's portrayal of the gods as being vengeful and untrustworthy would not be tolerated. The violence Americans see daily, whether via Hollywood movies, school shootings, or video games, would be as well, as Plato believed it would have the effect of normalizing it, hence making it acceptable. Even though the producer class had the least restrictions placed upon them, Plato planned regulation of "getting" or accumulating wealth, believing that without wealth regulation, the more industrious producers would get richer while the less motivated got poorer, ultimately resulting in conflict.

[**Professor**] Western democracies have safeguards against politicians who abuse power or are inept or corrupt. Every two years, voters can vote them out of office and elect new ones. How could Plato guarantee his philosopher kings would not be corrupted by absolute power, and if they were, what could be done about it?

Like all totalitarian and authoritarian governments, there were no safeguards or alternative plans to remedy the situation because Plato did not think they were necessary. The idea was to design a conflict-free society presided over by guardians impervious to the lure of power and only concerned with knowledge and truth. Despite Plato's significance as the primary source of the rationalist tradition in Western civilization, the flaw in his logic was the Socratic dictum that no one ever does wrong intentionally. Any instance of wrongdoing or immorality was a simple matter of an individual's ignorance. If someone knows what is good, they will always act in such a manner as to achieve it. Some people agree with Socrates and his view that "no man knowingly does evil." We can both agree that this is simply untrue. As St. Paul said, "For I do not do the good I want, but the evil I do not want is what I do."

[**Professor**] I'm starting to understand your point regarding the government of the United States transforming into a sinister and perverted version of Plato's Republic.

Please elaborate.

[**Professor**] For one thing, I would equate Plato's philosopher-king or guardian class to the office of the President of the United States.

You would be correct in your view.

[**Professor**] The rigor and commitment to knowledge that Plato required for a person in this position does not exist today. Just because someone can run a successful business does not qualify them to run America and, by extension, the world. No matter how decorated or famous, actors, businesspeople, and military figures should not be entrusted with such power unless they can prove they deserve it. It is frightening to me that some Americans think Kid Rock would be a great president. Moreover, it is evident that despite Plato's desire for the inability of philosopher kings and the military class to acquire wealth and to live extravagantly, as this would conflict with their loyalty to Athens, we see something quite different in the United States. The political class has merged with the military and corporate America, using this alliance for personal gain. Their efforts are financed by the producer class, which corresponds with the modern-day middle class.

You have just described what modern-day political theorists describe as the military-industrial complex.

[**Professor**] Like Plato's Republic, I agree that much state-sponsored propaganda and censorship exists in the United States. Ideas that deviated from the progressive political narrative were branded as disinformation by many in the media and academia during the Biden administration.

The view that America is irredeemable and built on systemic racism and slavery is a central feature of the propaganda. I know you feel strongly about white supremacy and systemic racism and feel they are more prevalent than ever. Let's agree to disagree on that point. I concede America's legacy of slavery is a dagger to the illusions of ourselves as a nation. That said, whether we speak of human rights, LGBTQ rights, women's rights, animal rights, and almost every right imaginable, I assert that all of the above are better off than they were seventy years ago. There is no place where marginalized groups are better off than in the United States. Earlier, you argued that in Plato's Republic, there were no guarantees that philosopher kings would not be corrupted by wielding such absolute power and no provisions to remove them from power if they did.

Another problem with philosopher-kings as rulers is that there would be harmony among those in the guardian class, and they would have the same ideas on how to govern best. Philosophy did not stop with Plato, and conflict came immediately with Aristotle. Plato and Aristotle had fundamentally different visions of the world, just like liberals and conservatives do today. Aristotle rejected the political absolutism and the speculative and utopian ideals of The Republic, even though philosophers were in charge. Plato designed the ideal type of government, which Athens had to conform to, but Aristotle raised a new question: What type of government was best and most workable?

He did this by examining and building upon the ideals expressed in existing states' laws, customs, and public opinion. Aristotle was not a builder of utopias.

[**Professor**] I will get to the heart of the matter because we are deviating from why we are here today. You were observed after class on the steps of Low Library, conversing with your Social Theory class classmates, who were half your age, and your words were hostile, even terroristic. On the other hand, I admit that I was not present. Your Professor lectured about Francis Fukuyama's view that liberal democracy was "the end point of man's ideological evolution." Fukuyama asserted that liberal democracy was the best system of governance, and it rested upon three pillars: the rule of law, political accountability, and, most notably, a strong and effective state. You also defended President Trump. Do you remember this event? Speak now, for this is your chance to clear your name.

I remember the day in question. It was the highlight of my time at Columbia University. Please understand that I was not teaching or lecturing them but questioning them. That's a big difference and central to my defense. They gathered around me that day, eager to hear my views on Hans-Hermann Hoppe, of whom our Professor was unaware. Hoppe rejected Fukuyama's thesis that the final form of government was based on one man/one-vote rule by the people and that once this was achieved, history, at least as far as government was concerned, ended. Hoppe believed that democracy, as practiced today, is inferior to monarchy as a method of governance. Of course, he concluded that a private law society was the best method of governance.

[**Professor**] I'm not sure I understand what you mean by as practiced today. Are you referring to Donald Trump's attack on democracy at the Capitol Building **on January 6th?**

While the events of January 6th were indefensible, I discussed two things with my classmates that I felt were the more significant threats to democracy in the United States. The first was the transfer of governmental decision-making into the hands of unaccountable private power. The second was the idea that a method of legalized corruption (lobbyists, campaign contributions, and payoffs to powerful interests) had short-circuited the connection between voters and their representatives and weakened democracy far more than President Trump ever could. If that statement categorizes me as a defender of President Trump, then I am guilty as charged.

[**Professor**] We have seen the rise of Vladimir Putin and Xi Jinping and Britain's rejection of European-style liberalism manifested in Brexit. You don't see these events, which, by the way, corresponded with the rise of Donald Trump as a threat to liberal democracy worldwide? I just can't understand how oblivious you are when it's clear.

Let me first address your question about democracy as practiced today. One of Hoppe's main points about why monarchy was better than modern-day democracy was that the transition from monarchy to democracy involved replacing a king. Hoppe asserted that a king was a "permanent monopoly owner who owned the country, thus more discriminating, moderate, and future-oriented in his decisions" He argued that "because a king would bequeath his realm to his heirs or successors, he would care about the repercussions of his actions. In contrast, modern-day democracy is administered by "democratic caretakers (politicians) who don't own the country, therefore having no long-term interest in allegiance to it." Of course, Hoppe pointed out that "public officials running a democratic state can't, like kings, own foreign territory and the motive for waging war becomes ideological, waged on behalf of democracy, liberty, or any number of reasons."

[**Professor**] So, where does Donald Trump fit into this? Is he the savior of democracy? You haven't answered my question about the correlation between the rise of Donald Trump and the appeal of authoritarian regimes worldwide.

I see him as neither a savior of democracy nor an authoritarian dictator, as he is often portrayed. I only seek to understand the conditions that led to his rise to power and why many believe he has been treated more unfairly than any president in American history. Other wealthy business people who pledged to run America like a business have all tried and failed to garner the support of the American people. Why has Donald Trump succeeded where others have failed? Could it be because he's successfully conveyed how the Washington establishment is failing us better than his predecessors? It is an intriguing question I wanted to explore with my classmates, and as for democracy, we both agree that despite democracy firmly in place, the United States seems to be on the verge of civil war. Moreover, whether it comes to giving up their personal liberty, guns, or their ability to speak freely or be aggressively surveilled, Americans have been willing to relinquish power to the government without a fight. They were even willing to accept Kamala Harris as a possible candidate for President of the United States, even though she did not take part in the primary process and was foisted upon the American people in a scenario hitherto unknown.

President Trump's detractors portray his presidency as a modern-day version of the oligarchy of the Thirty Tyrants, complete with unsubstantiated claims that he is using his office for personal gain. His supporters make the identical claim against his enemies and that President Trump is trying to protect us from a bunch of left-wing zealot politicians, allegedly using their positions of power for personal profit while presiding over a surveillance state as their net worth increases tenfold after leaving office. World leaders have noticed the dissatisfaction and turmoil.

They are promoting alternatives to Western-style democracy, like China's "whole-process democracy", which I feel is Aristotelian in its concept in that it considers a country's history and culture and adapts it for use as a new way to govern. This form of governance, conceived from China's unique conditions and similar to Plato's Republic, is more concerned with how well the government can improve the socio-economic lives of its citizens and less concerned with the democratic process.

Taking the United States as an example, suppose the people's needs are unmet, and there is discord. In that case, it doesn't matter that an individual has the power to vote for a political candidate every two or four years if the people they elect continue to be ignorant of their needs. Singapore is another example of a country that straddles the line between a liberal democracy and an authoritarian regime; some call it an illiberal democracy, and others say it resembles China but a more sophisticated, less corrupt, and improved version. My friend moved there from the United States and says he approves of every aspect of how the country is run. The dysfunction of the United States government and liberal democracies is evident, and alternatives to it are coming onto the world stage as China poises itself to be the world's next great superpower. This dysfunction has nothing to do with President Trump and everything to do with the possible shortcomings of democracy, or perhaps more accurately, democracy gone astray.

[**Professor**] Whole process democracy does seem similar to the ideas Plato expressed in The Republic. However, I wouldn't suggest that Xi Jinping and the CCP are philosopher kings making decisions based on their lifelong study of virtue and knowledge.

I am not suggesting that China and Singapore are better alternatives to American liberal democracy. What I am asserting is that blaming Donald Trump alone for the worldwide anomie so prevalent today is unwise and inaccurate. Americans are starting to wise up to the "vote for me, and everything will be all right" scenario. Moreover, voters can use many alternatives to the mainstream media to educate themselves about their world. These alternatives and the ability to question authority would not have existed in Plato's Republic, and they do not exist in Russia, China, and many countries in the Middle East. This freedom of inquiry and open dialogue is the cornerstone of a free society. I have many colleagues in Russia, China, and the Middle East, and their governments censor them by restricting internet access and using tools like Signal, which enable encrypted conversations. The freedom individuals have in the United States to find out about the machinations of their government is what sets the United States apart. Still, this very freedom can cause a society to unravel, especially when those we elect to govern us betray us and, in many instances, have been lying to us for a very long time.

As a result, we are seeing an increase in censorship on platforms like YouTube, Facebook, and X. There is also an increase in self-censorship by individuals fearing repercussions from publicizing their views. In short, we are becoming more like the places we claim are repressive, and I am putting my life on the line to put an end to it. Professor Di Neve, as we near the end of this trial, and in keeping with the Socratic theme, I would like to reacquaint you with Socrates' words as presented in Plato's Apology, which serves as a prescient warning: "...you will not easily discover another of my sort, who-even if it is rather ridiculous to say- has simply been set upon the University by the God, as though upon a great and well-born horse who is rather sluggish because of his great size and needs to be awakened by some gadfly. O citizens of Trump's America and Professor Di Neve, I am grateful and your friend, but I will obey God rather than you, and as long as I draw breath and am able, I shall not cease to practice philosophy. I will not yield to any man or woman contrary to what is right, for fear of death, even if I should die at once for not yielding. For those considering convicting me, it is not I who is on trial today but the practice of philosophy and free inquiry. When I am gone, others will take my place. I am seventy years old, and my natural death is inevitable. If you convict me today, you will be condemned for your condemnation of me, and the next generation of truth seekers will replace me.

For those who plan to vote for my acquittal, please understand I have no fear of death, as it is better to die as an unjust person than to live as an unjust person. My pursuit of a rational and virtuous life has led me here today. Thus, death should not be feared by the righteous person. Human wisdom is admitting that we cannot know everything and to remain curious. We ought not to be concerned with death because fearing death involves thinking we know what we do not know. We ought to be concerned with the welfare of our souls. My life has been a testament to this mission. I have been implored to go into politics, but I knew that if I did, I would have to compromise my principles. All I have done is to go about persuading you, young and old alike, not to care for your bodies or your wealth so intensely as for the greatest well-being of your souls.

Young people of Trump's America, know that I am your ally, not your enemy. In my time at Columbia, I learned much from conversations with young students who helped me see things from a fresh new perspective, including Professor Di Neve, who clearly articulated why she felt the way she did, with poise and intelligence. Conversely, it was rewarding when I could do the same for students who were previously unaware of Austrian economics and libertarian ideas, making us consider our government's proper function. I hope my dialogue with the esteemed Professor Di Neve will be a jumping-off point for her further explorations. Should a government employ its citizens and provide social safety nets, offer student loans and free public education, or is the idea of a night watchman or minarchist state a better option? In the future, these are all crucial questions that won't be answered if I am convicted here today.

(Professor Di Neve realized that the exchange between herself and Adamantios was not only enjoyable but vital to the health and well-being of Western civilization. What started as a cross-examination became an engaging dialogue that surpassed the usual stereotypes. She asked the judge for a mistrial, which was granted, and dismissed the case against Adamantios. Di Neve asked to speak to the jury.)

[**Professor**] I want to start by apologizing to Adamantios for wishing him death. It was mean-spirited and unbefitting of a college administrator. As I said earlier, I am neither a Marxist nor a socialist. Still, Marx was absolutely correct when he asserted that the history of all hitherto existing society is the history of class struggles. Hegel stated that philosophy is "its own time comprehended in thoughts." In other words, philosophy reflects and understands the specific era in which it exists. It is a product of its time, not a timeless body of knowledge that comes too late for society to utilize the philosophic wisdom to transform it. Hegel viewed philosophy not as an objective pursuit of the truth but as a subjective interpretation of the world. I disagree with Adamantios' view that Plato's ideas are as relevant today as they were in his time. However, the

Socratic critical thinking method, exposing inconsistencies in one's beliefs and fostering a more profound understanding through questioning, is a valuable practice.

On the other hand, Marxian philosophy is as relevant today as ever. Before Marx, philosophers could only interpret the world, but as we learned in Theses on Feuerbach, the point should be to change it. Jean-Paul Sartre argued that Marxism was "the inescapable philosophy of our time, which we cannot go beyond because we have not gone beyond the circumstances that engendered it." Class conflict is key to understanding, as a top-down war is being waged against the working class. Adamantios is correct in arguing that unaccountable private power has tainted American democracy as it morphs into an oligarchy. Of course, the academics, journalists, politicians, and think tanks who derive sustenance from this unaccountable private power are unwilling to address it for obvious reasons. American citizens fail to understand the power they have in solidarity. In the United States, we fight over the right to abortion or to bear arms. We form our opinions on our fellow citizens based on their political party affiliation. Black athletes can kneel in protest during the national anthem or boldly publicly criticize the politicians of their choice. You can burn the American flag or even tell a sitting president to go fuck himself. This gives Americans the idea that they have power, but that power is illusory. The ability to do the above does little to address the problems of everyday Americans who can't buy a home or send their children to college and live paycheck to paycheck. None of the infighting and bickering affects the bottom line of the giant American multinational corporations playing a different game.

President Trump proudly proclaimed to a cheering Congress that the United States would never be a socialist or communist nation, even though socialism for wealthy bankers has existed for quite some time. Ronald Reagan bailed out Continental Illinois, the biggest bailout in American history at that time. He ended his term in office with another massive financial crisis, the Savings and Loan Crisis, which was followed by the Enron scandal. Finally, in 2008, Wall Street bankers were responsible for the near collapse of the global economy until the American taxpayer bailed them out. My neighbor, who attended trade school and started a lucrative construction business with his sons and knew I favored loan forgiveness, asked me how it was remotely fair to ask people who chose to forego a four-year degree in favor of mastering a skill that is in demand to pay off someone else's student loans. I wondered where his outrage was for the financial institutions that knew what they were doing was risky but had no reservations about declaring bankruptcy, taking billions in government bailouts, and walking away from the crisis they caused with millions.

On the other hand, neither I nor the thousands of students consciously decided to default on our student loans. When we filled out our FAFSA forms, we had to answer questions requiring a fundamental understanding of economics and how much debt we would carry. We had to check off a box agreeing to pay off our loan; otherwise, the application would not proceed. When student loans were temporarily suspended during the pandemic, and student loan forgiveness was discussed, we were grateful to accept what our government offered us. Unlike the Wall Street crew, college students were cast as pariahs by the usual suspects: the "government is the problem, not the solution" faction, who want the government to guarantee the success of business ventures of large corporations by taking away every perk that the working class gained since the New Deal. At the same time, the market principles they espouse only prevail for the working class.

The pundits from your favorite cable news shows are like the court intellectuals during the days of the monarchy, doing all they can to obfuscate what is truly going on by putting limits and restrictions on what can be discussed and pitting the working class against each other by dividing us up into liberals and conservatives, or globalists and progressives. In the days of monarchy, a king would ride through the village and toss coins to the downtrodden masses. I am tired of our leaders doing the same with empty words and gestures, thoughts and prayers, and no substantive action. The last thing that the mass media or the D.C. politicians want is unity between the young, blue-haired, radical feminist Columbia University student and the older Black American conservative and for Americans to think for themselves. While I still have fundamental disagreements with Adamantios, our interaction today was crucial. We must make a daily effort to replace ignorance with knowledge. We learn little by conversing with those who think exactly like us. We must retreat from our Bluesky and Truth Social echo chambers and instead discuss and debate with individuals whose worldview is a radical departure from ours. It is not sufficient to hold only our leaders accountable. We must be better by employing the Aristotelian concept of eudaimonia, the constant pursuit of excellence in all areas of life that will, in turn, make us all more excellent, functional, and happier. Most importantly, we must strive to question everyone and everything because, as Socrates told us over two thousand years ago, the unexamined life isn't worth living.